Cyber Wise

By

R. Allure

For all those lovely people who are interested...

Contents

CHAPTER 1

Intention:

My intention in the following writing was to create a small cyber security book for all types of readers. What you are about to read is written simply with examples of the types of scenarios and impacts.

Since I work in cyber security, and have realised it is a fast evolving field, I felt that a small book will provide insights into something that will potentially affect everyone. The reason for such a small book is that so many of us are time poor, yet I felt such a book could help people and provide an insight into something that many people have limited opportunity to learn about. Please enjoy.

CHAPTER 2

Introduction: Navigating the Digital Battleground

In the labyrinth of the digital era, where every keystroke leaves a trace and every click sends ripples across the vast expanse of cyberspace, the need for a vigilant guardian has never been more crucial. Welcome to the realm of "Cyber wise," a journey into the heart of cybersecurity, where the forces of innovation and threat converge in a perpetual dance.

In an age where our lives are intricately woven into the digital tapestry, cyber threats have transcended mere nuisances to become formidable adversaries, capable of disrupting the very fabric of our interconnected world. The importance of cybersecurity goes far beyond safeguarding data; it's about protecting the essence of our modern existence.

Why Cybersecurity Matters: Unravelling the Layers

Imagine a world where personal information is a treasure trove for malevolent actors, where critical infrastructure dances on the edge of vulnerability, and

where the boundaries between physical and virtual blur into a complex tapestry of risk. The 'why' behind cybersecurity is rooted in preserving the integrity of our digital infrastructure, ensuring privacy, and defending against the ever-evolving arsenal of cyber threats.

The Anatomy of Cyber Threats: Beyond the Surface

To navigate this digital battleground effectively, one must delve into the intricacies of cyber threats. "Cyber wise" unfolds the layers, exploring the techniques of reconnaissance, initial access, persistence, and the myriad phases of a cyber-attack. From the subtle art of privilege escalation to the clandestine world of command and control, each chapter unravels the tools and tactics employed by both adversaries and defenders.

Embark with us on this expedition into the world of cyber resilience. As we journey through the shadows of cyber threats, let "Cyber wise" be your guide, equipping you with the knowledge to understand, thwart, and ultimately triumph in the face of the digital adversaries that lurk in the virtual corridors of our interconnected existence. The voyage begins; are you ready to navigate the unseen challenges that lie ahead?

CHAPTER 3

The Evolution of Cybersecurity: A Journey Through Time

To understand where we are now with cyber security – here is a time line containing some major turning points and initiators of cyber concerns:

1960s - The Dawn of Cybersecurity

In the early days of computing, cybersecurity was a nascent concept, overshadowed by the sheer excitement of technological advancements. The first inklings of security concerns emerged as researchers like Robert Morris Sr. worked on Multics, a groundbreaking time-sharing operating system. These early pioneers laid the groundwork for future security measures.

1970s - Birth of Encryption and the First Computer Virus

The 1970s witnessed the birth of public-key cryptograph, a pivotal moment in securing communication. Whitfield Diffie and Martin Hellman introduced the concept of asymmetric encryption, paving the way for secure data transmission. However,

this era also saw the emergence of the first computer virus, the Creeper, highlighting the need for protection against malicious software.

1980s - Rise of Malware and the Morris Worm

The 1980s marked a turning point with the advent of personal computers. However, this newfound accessibility also opened doors to cyber threats. In 1988, the infamous Morris Worm, created by Robert Tappan Morris, became the first large-scale worm to infect the internet, causing widespread disruption and emphasising the necessity of security protocols.

1990s - Internet Boom and the Birth of Firewalls

As the internet proliferated, so did cyber threats. The 1990s witnessed a surge in cyber-attacks, prompting the development of firewalls to control network traffic. The "ILOVEYOU" worm in 2000 served as a wake-up call, demonstrating the destructive potential of social engineering in the digital age.

2000s - Proliferation of Cybercrime and Advanced Persistent Threats (APTs)

The 21st century brought a surge in cybercrime, with attacks evolving in sophistication. Notorious incidents,

such as the Stuxnet worm targeting Iran's nuclear program in 2010, showcased the potential for cyber-attacks to have geopolitical ramifications. The concept of Advanced Persistent Threats (APTs) gained prominence as persistent, stealthy attacks aimed at specific targets.

2010s - Dawn of the Internet of Things (IoT) Era

The advent of IoT introduced new challenges, expanding the attack surface. High-profile breaches, like the Equifax data breach in 2017, emphasised the need for robust cybersecurity measures to protect vast amounts of sensitive data. The development of bug bounty programs gained traction, encouraging ethical hackers to identify and patch vulnerabilities.

2020s - Cybersecurity in the Age of AI and Global Threats

In the current decade, cybersecurity faces unprecedented challenges with the integration of artificial intelligence and machine learning. The SolarWinds supply chain attack in 2020 underscored the potential impact of sophisticated attacks on a global scale, emphasising the need for collaborative defence strategies.

Today, cybersecurity stands as a dynamic and ever-evolving field, shaped by the lessons of the past and the ongoing commitment to staying one step ahead of emerging threats.

CHAPTER 4

Reconnaissance: Unveiling the Digital Footprints

In the intricate dance of cyber warfare, the initial phase often determines the success or failure of an impending attack. Reconnaissance, the art of gathering intelligence, has evolved into a sophisticated process of uncovering digital footprints, exposing vulnerabilities, and shaping the trajectory of a cyber offensive.

1. Open-Source Intelligence (OSINT) Gathering through Social Media:

Example: The LinkedIn Connection Chain

In an era where personal and professional lives intertwine online, social media platforms have become gold mines for cyber adversaries. Consider the case of a seemingly innocuous LinkedIn profile. By navigating through connections, an attacker can map an organisation's structure, identify key personnel, and understand internal relationships. This wealth of information becomes a roadmap for crafting targeted phishing campaigns or exploiting weak links within the organisational chain.

Repercussions: Increased Phishing Precision and Social Engineering Attacks

Armed with insights from social media reconnaissance, attackers can craft highly personalised phishing emails, making them indistinguishable from legitimate communications. The repercussions include an elevated risk of successful social engineering attacks, leading to unauthorised access, data breaches, and potential compromise of sensitive information.

2. DNS Enumeration using Tools like DNSDumpster:

Example: Mining DNS Information for Subdomain Discovery

Domain Name System (DNS) enumeration serves as a cornerstone in the reconnaissance phase. Tools like DNSDumpster allow cyber actors to efficiently map an organisation's digital presence by revealing subdomains, associated IP addresses, and other DNS-related details. This technique aids attackers in understanding the structure of target networks, facilitating the identification of potential entry points and weak spots.

Repercussions: Expanded Attack Surface and Targeted Exploitation

The repercussions of effective DNS enumeration are twofold. First, it expands the attack surface by uncovering often overlooked subdomains that may lack robust security measures. Second, armed with this information, attackers can pinpoint specific vulnerabilities associated with discovered subdomains, increasing the likelihood of successful exploitation and unauthorised access.

3. Network Scanning with Tools like Nmap:

Example: Uncovering Open Ports and Services

Nmap, a powerful network scanning tool, plays a pivotal role in reconnaissance by probing target systems for open ports and services. By identifying exposed services, attackers gain insights into potential attack vectors and weak points within the network architecture. Unsecured services become entry points for subsequent phases of the cyber kill chain.

Repercussions: Enhanced Attack Planning and Exploitation

The information gleaned from network scanning empowers attackers to refine their attack strategies.

Understanding the network's topology and exposed services allows for meticulous planning, ensuring that subsequent attack vectors align with the identified vulnerabilities. This increases the efficiency of exploitation, potentially leading to unauthorised access, data compromise, or disruption of critical services.

In the complex dance between defenders and adversaries, the reconnaissance phase sets the stage for the cybersecurity battle. As organisations strive to fortify their digital defences, a nuanced understanding of reconnaissance techniques becomes imperative to thwart the ever-evolving threats that lurk in the shadows of the virtual realm.

CHAPTER 5

Resource Development: Unearthing the Arsenal

Resource development in the realm of cyber warfare involves the strategic acquisition and cultivation of assets that adversaries exploit to maximise the impact of their attacks. This phase, marked by its subtlety and cunning, lays the groundwork for a spectrum of cyber offenses, from phishing campaigns to targeted intrusions.

1. Domain Squatting and Typosquatting for Phishing Campaigns:

Example: Mimicking Legitimate Domains for Deception

Imagine a scenario where an unsuspecting user mistypes a commonly visited website address. Cyber adversaries capitalise on this human error through domain squatting and typosquatting, creating deceptive domains that closely resemble legitimate ones. For instance, substituting a common "l" with an uppercase "I" or appending an extra letter can go unnoticed by hurried users.

Impacts and Outcomes: Deceptive Lures and Credential Harvesting

The impact of such tactics is profound. Users, thinking they are accessing a trusted site, may unknowingly submit sensitive credentials, providing attackers with a gateway to unauthorised access. Phishing campaigns leveraging these deceptive domains can lead to compromised accounts, unauthorised data access, and potential financial losses.

Combat Strategies: Active Domain Monitoring and User Education

Combatting domain squatting involves active monitoring of domain registrations, identification of suspicious patterns, and prompt takedown of malicious domains. User education plays a crucial role, with organisations emphasising the importance of scrutinising website URLs and being cautious of subtle variations.

2. Scraping Websites for Employee Information:

Example: Harvesting Employee Data for Targeted Attacks

In the resource development phase, cyber adversaries often turn to web scraping as a means to compile a treasure trove of information about an organisation's employees. By extracting details from public websites, forums, or social media, attackers construct profiles that enable them to craft highly targeted and convincing spear-phishing campaigns.

Impacts and Outcomes: Precision Targeting and Social Engineering

The impacts of scraping employee information are twofold. First, it enables attackers to tailor phishing messages with specific details, making them more convincing. Second, the gathered intelligence aids in crafting socially engineered attacks, exploiting personal and professional connections to increase the likelihood of success.

Combat Strategies: Data Minimisation and Security Awareness Training

Organisations combatting this threat focus on data minimisation, reducing the public exposure of sensitive employee information. Security awareness training emphasises the importance of cautious online behaviour and recognising potential social engineering attempts, fostering a culture of cybersecurity vigilance.

Resource development, with its nuanced tactics, underscores the need for organisations to fortify their defences against the subtle intricacies of cyber threats. As defenders evolve their strategies, a comprehensive approach that blends technology, vigilance, and education becomes paramount in mitigating the risks associated with this intricate phase of the cyber kill chain.

CHAPTER 6

Initial Access: Breaching the Gates

The initial access phase marks the point of no return for cyber adversaries as they breach an organisation's defences. This critical juncture often involves exploiting human vulnerabilities through sophisticated social engineering or leveraging technical weaknesses in software. Let's delve into two prevalent methods: phishing attacks and the exploitation of software vulnerabilities.

1. Phishing Attacks (e.g., Spear-Phishing Emails):

Common Scenario: The Deceptive Lure

In a spear-phishing scenario, an attacker crafts a tailored email designed to deceive a specific individual or group within an organisation. The message may appear authentic, often masquerading as a trusted entity such as a colleague, superior, or a reputable service provider. The email typically contains a compelling call to action, enticing the recipient to click on a malicious link, download an infected attachment, or divulge sensitive information.

Suspicious Indicators: What to Look For

Individuals should remain vigilant for red flags such as unexpected emails requesting sensitive information, urgent requests that create a sense of panic, or emails with unusual grammar and formatting. Hovering over hyperlinks without clicking can reveal deceptive URLs. Security awareness and training programs play a crucial role in educating personnel on identifying these indicators.

Sequence of Events: From Deception to Breach

Upon falling victim to a phishing attack, the sequence of events can be swift. Clicking on a malicious link may lead to the installation of malware, compromising the user's device. Stolen credentials can provide access to sensitive systems, and the attacker may move laterally within the network, escalating privileges and potentially exfiltrating valuable data.

Costs and Implications: Financial Loss and Reputational Damage

The costs associated with a successful phishing attack extend beyond immediate financial losses. Organisations may suffer reputational damage, loss of customer trust, and potential legal consequences. Remediation efforts, including incident response,

system restoration, and enhanced cybersecurity measures, further escalate the overall impact.

2. Exploiting Software Vulnerabilities (e.g., Exploiting Unpatched Systems):

Common Scenario: Targeting the Weakest Link

Exploiting unpatched systems involves identifying and capitalising on vulnerabilities in software that have not been updated with the latest security patches. Attackers actively seek out organisations with outdated or poorly maintained systems, probing for weaknesses that grant them unauthorised access.

Suspicious Indicators: Identifying Vulnerable Systems

Regular system updates and patch management are crucial in preventing exploitation. Signs of vulnerable systems include delayed or neglected patching processes, irregular system behaviour, or a sudden increase in system vulnerabilities reported by security assessments.

Sequence of Events: From Vulnerability to Compromise

Once a vulnerability is identified, attackers exploit it to gain initial access. The sequence may involve deploying malware, establishing a foothold, and gradually escalating privileges. The compromised system then

becomes a launchpad for further exploration and exploitation within the organisation's network.

Costs and Implications: Operational Disruption and Legal Consequences

The consequences of exploiting software vulnerabilities can be severe. Operational disruptions, data breaches, and the compromise of critical systems can lead to significant financial losses. Organisations may face legal repercussions, especially if sensitive customer or employee data is compromised.

In the cat-and-mouse game of cybersecurity, understanding the intricacies of the initial access phase is paramount. Proactive measures, including robust training, regular software patching, and a comprehensive cybersecurity strategy, serve as the frontline defences against the potential fallout from successful initial access attacks.

CHAPTER 7

Execution: Unleashing the Cyber Arsenal

The execution phase represents the moment when cyber adversaries deploy their weapons to carry out the intended attack. In this phase, we'll explore two common methods: malware execution through malicious attachments and code injection attacks targeting web applications.

1. Malware Execution Through Malicious Attachments:

Example: The Weaponised Attachment

In this scenario, adversaries send emails containing seemingly harmless attachments, such as documents or spreadsheets. These attachments, however, harbour malicious payloads. For instance, a Word document may contain a macro that, when enabled, triggers the download and execution of malware onto the victim's system.

Indicators: Recognising Suspicious Attachments

Users should be cautious when receiving unexpected emails with attachments, especially if they prompt the enabling of macros or other executable content. Unusual file extensions, misspellings in the email

content, or unexpected sender addresses can serve as indicators of a potential malicious attachment.

Repercussions: Compromised Systems and Data Theft

 Once the malicious attachment is opened, the embedded malware executes on the victim's system. The consequences can range from system compromise to data theft, with the potential for unauthorised access, ransomware deployment, or the establishment of a persistent presence within the network.

2. Code Injection Attacks Targeting Web Applications:

Example: Exploiting Vulnerabilities in Web Code

Web applications often process user input, and code injection attacks exploit vulnerabilities in this process. For instance, SQL injection involves injecting malicious SQL code into user inputs, tricking the application into executing unintended database queries. Similarly, cross-site scripting (XSS) allows attackers to inject malicious scripts into web pages viewed by other users.

Indicators: Unusual Website Behaviour and Error Messages

Users may observe unexpected behaviours on websites, such as the display of error messages or the appearance of unauthorised content. Web administrators should monitor for unusual traffic patterns, unexpected database queries, or an influx of suspicious user inputs.

Repercussions: Compromised User Data and System Control

Successful code injection attacks can lead to the compromise of sensitive data stored in databases, unauthorised access to user accounts, or even full control over web servers. Attackers may use these exploits to deface websites, steal user credentials, or pivot further into an organisation's internal network.

In the execution phase, understanding the tactics employed by cyber adversaries is crucial for building effective defences. Robust email filtering, user education on recognising phishing attempts, and regular security audits for web applications are vital components of a proactive cybersecurity strategy. As organisations fortify their defences against execution-based attacks, they thwart the malicious actors seeking to exploit vulnerabilities for their nefarious objectives.

CHAPTER 8

Persistence: The Silent Occupation

The persistence phase of a cyber-attack is akin to the adversary establishing a foothold within the compromised environment, ensuring continued access and control. This strategic phase involves methods such as creating backdoors in compromised systems and utilising registry persistence on Windows systems.

1. Backdoors in Compromised Systems:

How It Plays Out: Establishing Covert Entry Points

Backdoors are clandestine pathways created by attackers to maintain access to a compromised system without detection. Once initial access is achieved, adversaries often deploy backdoors to secure a persistent presence. This involves installing malicious software or manipulating existing functionalities to enable covert communication channels.

Indicators: Unusual Network Traffic and Suspicious Processes

Detecting backdoors can be challenging, but indicators include unusual outbound network traffic, unexpected

system behaviour, or the presence of unfamiliar processes running in the background. Regular network monitoring and anomaly detection are crucial in identifying these subtle signs.

Real-Time Example: The ShadowPad Backdoor

The ShadowPad backdoor, discovered in 2017, infiltrated software used by various organisations globally. It allowed attackers to execute arbitrary code, providing them with persistent access. The backdoor was concealed within legitimate software updates, highlighting the need for vigilance even with trusted sources.

Repercussions: Prolonged Unauthorised Access and Data Compromise

 The repercussions of successful backdoor deployment are profound. Attackers can maintain prolonged access to compromised systems, silently observing and potentially escalating their privileges. This persistence amplifies the risk of data compromise, lateral movement, and other advanced attack techniques.

2. Registry Persistence on Windows Systems:

How It Plays Out: Manipulating System Registries

Windows systems use registries to store configuration settings and system information. In the persistence phase, adversaries manipulate these registries to ensure their malicious code or backdoors are executed every time the system starts. This can involve creating registry entries, modifying existing ones, or exploiting legitimate autostart mechanisms.

Indicators: Unusual Registry Changes and Suspicious Autostart Entries

 Monitoring for unexpected changes in the system's registry, especially those related to autostart entries, is crucial for detecting registry persistence techniques. Security tools and regular audits can help identify unauthorised modifications that may indicate the presence of persistent threats.

Real-Time Example: Stuxnet's Use of Registry Persistence

The Stuxnet worm, discovered in 2010, employed registry persistence as part of its sophisticated attack on Iran's nuclear program. Stuxnet manipulated Windows registries to ensure its components were

launched during system start-up, allowing it to maintain a persistent presence on infected systems.

Repercussions: Sustained Control and Potential for Advanced Attacks

Registry persistence grants attackers sustained control over compromised systems. Beyond maintaining access, this persistence is a crucial stepping stone for launching more advanced attack techniques, such as privilege escalation, lateral movement, and data exfiltration.

In the persistence phase, defenders face the challenge of identifying and removing hidden footholds that adversaries establish within the network. Continuous monitoring, threat hunting, and a robust incident response plan are essential components of a proactive cybersecurity strategy to mitigate the risks associated with persistent threats.

CHAPTER 9

Privilege Escalation: Ascending the Cyber Ladder

Privilege escalation is a pivotal phase in a cyber-attack where adversaries aim to acquire higher levels of access within a compromised environment. This phase involves exploiting misconfigurations, abusing weak user permissions, and employing other common techniques to elevate privileges.

1. Exploiting Misconfigurations for Privilege Escalation:

How It's Used: Capitalising on System Weaknesses

Adversaries often target misconfigurations in operating systems, applications, or network settings to exploit vulnerabilities and elevate their privileges. This can involve exploiting insecure default settings, improperly configured access controls, or overlooked security configurations that inadvertently grant excessive privileges.

Detection Strategies: Continuous Monitoring and Configuration Audits

Detecting misconfiguration-based privilege escalation requires continuous monitoring and regular configuration audits. Anomalies in system configurations, unexpected changes, or deviations from security baselines can be indicators of potential misconfiguration exploits.

Real-Life Example: Apache Struts Remote Code Execution

In the Equifax data breach of 2017, attackers exploited a misconfiguration in Apache Struts, a popular web application framework. By taking advantage of a known vulnerability, they gained unauthorised access and escalated privileges, ultimately leading to the exfiltration of sensitive data.

Outcomes: Unauthorised Access and Data Compromise

Successful exploitation of misconfigurations allows attackers to bypass normal access controls and gain elevated privileges. This can result in unauthorised access to critical systems, data compromise, and the potential for further lateral movement within the network.

2. Abusing Weak User Permissions to Gain Higher Access:

How It's Used: Leveraging Inadequate Access Controls

Adversaries may exploit weak user permissions by abusing legitimate access granted to users within the organisation. This can involve escalating privileges by exploiting vulnerabilities in applications or systems that are accessible to a user with lower-level permissions.

Detection Strategies: User Behaviour Analytics and Anomaly Detection

Detecting the abuse of weak user permissions requires monitoring user behaviour, especially deviations from typical patterns. Anomaly detection, combined with user behaviour analytics, helps identify unusual or suspicious activities that may indicate privilege escalation attempts.

Real-Life Example: Target's HVAC Vendor Attack

In the Target data breach of 2013, attackers gained initial access through a third-party HVAC vendor. Exploiting weak vendor credentials, they escalated their privileges, moving laterally within the network and eventually compromising point-of-sale systems.

Outcomes: Lateral Movement and Targeted Exploitation

Abusing weak user permissions enables attackers to move laterally within the network, potentially accessing sensitive systems and data. The outcomes may include the compromise of additional user accounts, privilege escalation to critical systems, and the execution of advanced attack techniques.

3. Other Common Techniques:

- Pass-the-Hash Attacks: Adversaries obtain hashed user credentials and use them to authenticate without needing to decrypt the actual passwords.

- DLL Injection: Injecting malicious code into running processes to gain control or escalate privileges.

- Kernel Exploits: Leveraging vulnerabilities in the operating system's kernel to escalate privileges.

Understanding and mitigating privilege escalation threats require a multi-faceted approach, including proactive security configuration management, continuous monitoring, and user education. As defenders fortify their systems against these techniques, they mitigate the risk of unauthorised access and minimise the potential impact of privilege escalation in a cyber-attack.

CHAPTER 10

Defence Evasion: Navigating Through the Shadows

In the cat-and-mouse game of cybersecurity, defence evasion represents the art of avoiding detection and circumventing security measures. Adversaries employ a variety of techniques, including signature evasion using polymorphic malware and disabling security software or services, to slip through the defences undetected.

1. Signature Evasion using Polymorphic Malware:

How It Looks: Constantly Shifting Facades

Polymorphic malware is designed to change its appearance with each iteration while retaining its malicious functionality. This constant mutation thwarts traditional signature-based detection systems, as each variant appears unique, making it difficult for antivirus programs to recognise the evolving malicious code.

Defence Strategies: Behaviour-Based Detection and Heuristic Analysis

Recognising the limitations of signature-based approaches, modern security solutions employ behaviour-based detection and heuristic analysis. These methods focus on identifying patterns of malicious behaviour rather than relying solely on static signatures, enabling the detection of polymorphic malware based on its actions.

Real-Time Example: Conficker Worm

The Conficker worm, first identified in 2008, utilised polymorphic techniques to continually change its code and avoid detection by traditional antivirus signatures. Its ability to mutate made it a persistent threat, highlighting the challenges of combating polymorphic malware.

Repercussions: Prolonged Infection and Increased Complexity

The use of polymorphic malware extends the time window during which an adversary can maintain control over compromised systems. The constant evolution of code introduces complexity, making it more challenging for security teams to develop effective countermeasures.

2. Disabling Security Software or Services:

How It Looks: Undermining the Watchdogs

Adversaries may attempt to disable or manipulate security software and services on a compromised system to create an environment conducive to their operations. This could involve stopping antivirus processes, altering firewall rules, or disabling security-related services.

Defence Strategies: Endpoint Protection and Continuous Monitoring

Endpoint protection solutions often include self-defence mechanisms to prevent unauthorised alterations to their processes. Continuous monitoring for unexpected changes to security configurations and regular integrity checks help detect and remediate instances where security software or services are compromised.

Real-Time Example: NotPetya Ransomware

The NotPetya ransomware, which wreaked havoc in 2017, employed techniques to disable security software on infected systems. By disabling security mechanisms, the malware had a greater chance of spreading rapidly and causing widespread damage.

Repercussions: Unimpeded Operations and Increased Damage

Disabling security software provides attackers with an unimpeded path to execute their operations. Without the watchful eye of security tools, adversaries can move laterally, escalate privileges, and carry out their malicious objectives with reduced interference.

3. Other Common Techniques:

Living Off the Land (LOL) Tactics: Leveraging legitimate system tools and processes to carry out malicious activities, making detection more challenging.

Encryption of Malicious Payloads: Encrypting or obfuscating malicious code to evade signature-based detection.

Zero-Day Exploits: Targeting vulnerabilities unknown to security vendors to bypass existing defences.

As adversaries continually refine their evasion tactics, defenders must adopt a proactive and dynamic security posture. This includes embracing advanced detection methods, threat intelligence, and a robust incident response plan to swiftly identify and neutralise threats before significant damage occurs.

CHAPTER 11

Credential Access: Unlocking the Gateways

Credential access is a critical phase in the cyber kill chain where attackers seek to obtain valid authentication credentials, unlocking access to sensitive systems and data. This phase involves various techniques, including password spraying attacks, keylogging, and credential theft through malware.

1. Password Spraying Attacks:

How It Looks: Subtle Yet Systematic

Password spraying is a stealthy technique where attackers systematically attempt a few commonly used passwords across a large number of user accounts. Unlike brute-force attacks that target a single account with multiple password attempts, password spraying is more subtle, avoiding lockout mechanisms.

Real-Life Example: The LinkedIn Data Breach (2012)

In the LinkedIn data breach of 2012, attackers used a combination of password spraying and data breaches

from other sources to gain access to user accounts. The compromised passwords were then used to access corporate networks and email accounts.

Repercussions: Unauthorised Access and Data Exposure

Successful password spraying can lead to unauthorised access to user accounts. The repercussions include potential data exposure, unauthorised information retrieval, and the ability for attackers to move laterally within the network.

Defence Strategies: Multi-Factor Authentication (MFA) and Account Lockout Policies

Implementing multi-factor authentication (MFA) adds an extra layer of security, even if passwords are compromised. Account lockout policies can also thwart password spraying by preventing repeated login attempts.

2. Keylogging or Credential Theft through Malware:

How It Looks: Silent Observers in the System

Keyloggers are malicious tools that capture keystrokes, including usernames and passwords, without the user's knowledge. Credential theft through malware involves

various methods, such as injecting code into legitimate processes to intercept login credentials.

Real-Life Example: Zeus Trojan

The Zeus Trojan, discovered in 2007, was notorious for its ability to steal sensitive information, including login credentials. It often targeted online banking users, capturing keystrokes and compromising financial accounts.

Repercussions: Compromised Identities and Financial Loss

Keylogging and credential theft through malware can lead to compromised identities, unauthorised access to sensitive accounts, and financial loss. Stolen credentials can be used for various malicious activities, including fraudulent transactions.

Defence Strategies: Endpoint Security and Regular Malware Scans

Robust endpoint security solutions that include anti-malware features can help detect and prevent keyloggers and other credential theft malware. Regular scans for malware and keeping software up to date are essential defence measures.

3. Other Common Techniques:

- Credential Sniffing on Networks: Monitoring network traffic to capture plaintext credentials.

- Brute-Force Attacks: Repeatedly attempting different password combinations until the correct one is found.

- Credential Stuffing: Using previously compromised usernames and passwords to gain unauthorised access to other accounts where users have reused credentials.

Credential access is a persistent challenge, and defenders must employ a combination of proactive measures to mitigate the risks associated with these techniques. This includes user education, strong password policies, multi-factor authentication, and the deployment of advanced endpoint security solutions. Regular monitoring and prompt incident response are crucial elements of a comprehensive defence strategy.

CHAPTER 12

Discovery: Unveiling the Digital Terrain

Discovery is a pivotal phase where cyber adversaries survey the digital landscape to identify assets, understand network configurations, and pinpoint vulnerabilities. In this phase, active techniques such as Active Directory reconnaissance and network mapping using tools like Wireshark play a crucial role.

1. Active Directory Reconnaissance:

How It Unfolds: Mapping Organisational Structure

Active Directory (AD) reconnaissance involves mapping an organisation's structure, users, groups, and relationships within the AD environment. Attackers aim to understand the hierarchical structure, privilege levels, and potential avenues for lateral movement.

Indicators: Unusual Queries and Anomalous Activity

Detecting Active Directory reconnaissance requires monitoring for unusual queries or requests within the AD environment. Anomalous activity, such as an excessive number of failed login attempts or unusual

privilege escalation patterns, may indicate reconnaissance attempts.

Approach: Continuous Monitoring and User Behaviour Analytics

Defending against AD reconnaissance involves continuous monitoring of AD logs, scrutinising user behaviour, and implementing user behaviour analytics. Recognising patterns associated with reconnaissance activities can help organisations identify and mitigate potential threats.

Interesting Fact: BloodHound Tool

BloodHound is a popular open-source tool used for Active Directory reconnaissance. It visualises the relationships and attack paths within an AD environment, providing both defenders and attackers with insights into potential vulnerabilities.

2. Network Mapping Using Tools like Wireshark:

How It Works: Unveiling the Network Topology

Network mapping involves using tools like Wireshark to capture and analyse network traffic, revealing the topology, devices, and communication patterns within

a network. Adversaries use this information to identify potential entry points and vulnerable systems.

Indicators: Unusual Network Traffic and Scanning Patterns

Detecting network mapping activities requires monitoring for unusual network traffic patterns, especially those indicative of scanning or reconnaissance. Sudden spikes in traffic, port scans, or unusual communication between devices may signal network mapping attempts.

Approach: Intrusion Detection Systems and Regular Traffic Analysis

Intrusion Detection Systems (IDS) play a crucial role in identifying network mapping activities. Regular analysis of network traffic, coupled with anomaly detection, enables defenders to spot unusual patterns and respond swiftly.

Interesting Fact: Wireshark's Protocol Analyser

Wireshark, a widely used network protocol analyser, allows security professionals to capture and inspect data traveling back and forth on a network in real time. While it's an invaluable tool for legitimate network

analysis, adversaries may exploit it for reconnaissance purposes.

3. Other Interesting Techniques/Situations:

- Service Enumeration: Identifying services running on network hosts to understand potential vulnerabilities.

- Google Dorking (Google Hacking): Using advanced search queries to discover sensitive information exposed on the internet.

- Internet-Wide Scanning: Conducting large-scale scans of the internet to identify vulnerable systems.

Inspiration for the Reader:

Discovery is a double-edged sword – while attackers seek to uncover vulnerabilities, defenders can leverage the same techniques to fortify their digital fortresses. The constant evolution of tools and techniques in this phase emphasises the need for organisations to stay vigilant, continuously adapt, and foster a culture of proactive cybersecurity.

By understanding the methods employed in the discovery phase, readers can gain insights into the dynamic nature of cybersecurity. It's a reminder that

defence requires not only robust technological solutions but also a keen understanding of the adversary's mind-set and strategic thinking.

CHAPTER 13

Lateral Movement: Navigating the Network Maze

Lateral movement is a strategic phase in the cyber-attack lifecycle where adversaries, having gained an initial foothold, seek to move laterally within the network to expand their influence and access. Techniques involved in lateral movement include exploiting trust relationships within networks, using compromised credentials, and various other methods.

1. Exploiting Trust Relationships within Networks:

How It Unfolds: Subverting Trust for Access

Adversaries exploit trust relationships between systems or users within a network to gain access to additional resources. This may involve leveraging the trust inherent in established connections, such as between workstations and servers or between trusted domains.

Indicators: Unusual Account Activity and Abnormal Resource Access

Detecting lateral movement through trust exploitation requires monitoring for unusual account activity, such as unexpected access to resources or authentication attempts from unexpected sources. Anomalies in lateral connections can be indicative of trust-based lateral movement.

Repercussions: Escalated Privileges and Compromised Resources

Successful exploitation of trust relationships can lead to escalated privileges and expanded access within the network. The repercussions may include unauthorised access to sensitive data, increased potential for further compromise, and a more challenging remediation process.

2. Using Compromised Credentials for Lateral Movement:

How It Works: Pivoting from Compromised Accounts

Adversaries often use compromised credentials obtained in earlier phases of the attack to move laterally within the network. This may involve using

stolen usernames and passwords or leveraging access tokens acquired through successful credential theft.

Indicators: Anomalous User Behaviour and Multiple Authentication Failures

Detecting lateral movement through compromised credentials requires monitoring for anomalous user behaviour, such as sudden access to new resources or systems. Multiple authentication failures or login attempts from different locations may indicate lateral movement attempts.

Repercussions: Widened Attack Surface and Increased Damage Potential

Lateral movement using compromised credentials extends the attacker's reach within the network, potentially leading to the compromise of additional systems and sensitive data. The increased attack surface raises the stakes for defenders in terms of potential damage and data exposure.

3. Other Techniques:

- Pass-the-Ticket Attacks: Exploiting Kerberos tickets for unauthorised access to systems.

- Remote Code Execution: Executing code on remote systems to establish a foothold.

- Man-in-the-Middle (MitM) Attacks: Intercepting and altering communications between systems for unauthorised access.

Indicators and Defence Strategies:

- Network Segmentation: Segregating network segments to limit lateral movement opportunities.

- Behavioural Analysis: Employing user and entity behaviour analytics (UEBA) to detect abnormal patterns.

- Intrusion Detection Systems (IDS): Utilising IDS to identify suspicious lateral movement activities.

Repercussions and Mitigation:

Lateral movement increases the potential impact of a cyber-attack by enabling adversaries to traverse and exploit various parts of the network. Effective mitigation involves a combination of proactive measures, including regular security training, network

segmentation, robust access controls, and continuous monitoring for unusual activity.

Takeaway for the Reader:

Understanding lateral movement is crucial for defenders seeking to thwart advanced cyber threats. The dynamic nature of lateral movement techniques emphasises the need for a comprehensive cybersecurity strategy that blends technological solutions with user awareness and proactive monitoring.

CHAPTER 14

Collection: Harvesting the Digital Bounty

The collection phase marks the culmination of a cyber-attack, where adversaries focus on extracting valuable information from compromised systems. Techniques in this phase include data exfiltration through covert channels, as well as the direct harvesting of sensitive information from compromised systems.

1. Data Exfiltration Through Covert Channels:

How It Operates: Stealthy Extraction of Stolen Data

Adversaries employ covert channels to exfiltrate stolen data without raising suspicion. These channels can include encrypted communication methods or leveraging seemingly innocuous protocols to transfer sensitive information undetected.

Real-Life Example: SolarWinds Supply Chain Attack (2020)

In the SolarWinds supply chain attack, threat actors compromised the software supply chain, embedding malicious code in the widely used SolarWinds Orion platform. The covertly exfiltrated data included

sensitive information from government agencies and major corporations.

Impacts: Systemic Breach and National Security Concerns

Covert data exfiltration in the SolarWinds attack had far-reaching consequences, compromising the security of multiple organisations and raising concerns about the integrity of critical infrastructure. The breach underscored the potential for systemic risks posed by sophisticated supply chain attacks.

Potential Long-Term Repercussions: Regulatory Scrutiny and Industry Trust Erosion

The SolarWinds attack led to increased regulatory scrutiny, with investigations into how such a significant breach occurred. The incident also contributed to a re-evaluation of trust in software supply chains, impacting how organisations approach vendor relationships.

2. Harvesting Sensitive Information from Compromised Systems:

How It Unfolds: Direct Extraction of Valuable Data

Adversaries may directly harvest sensitive information from compromised systems, including credentials, financial data, or proprietary business information. This can involve exploiting vulnerabilities, accessing databases, or extracting data stored on compromised devices.

Real-Life Example: Equifax Data Breach (2017)

In the Equifax data breach, attackers exploited a vulnerability in the Apache Struts web application to gain access to sensitive information, including personal details and credit data of millions of individuals. The harvested data had significant implications for individuals' financial security.

Impacts: Financial Losses and Identity Theft Risks

The Equifax breach resulted in financial losses for the affected individuals, with the compromised data providing a treasure trove for potential identity theft and fraudulent activities. The incident highlighted the broader impact of direct data harvesting on individuals' lives.

Potential Long-Term Repercussions: Legal Actions and Trust Erosion

Equifax faced legal actions, regulatory fines, and an erosion of trust from the public and industry partners. The incident spurred discussions about the responsibility of organisations to secure sensitive data and the need for robust cybersecurity practices.

3. Other Techniques:

- Clipboard Hijacking: Capturing data copied to the clipboard, including usernames and passwords.

- Memory Scraping: Extracting sensitive information from a system's memory, often targeting running processes.

- Brute-Force Attacks: Repeated attempts to decrypt or access encrypted data by trying various combinations.

Mitigation Strategies:

- Data Loss Prevention (DLP): Implementing DLP solutions to monitor and control the movement of sensitive data.

- Encryption: Encrypting sensitive data to protect it from unauthorised access even if systems are compromised.

- Behavioural Analytics: Leveraging behavioural analysis to detect anomalous data access patterns.

Takeaway for the Reader:

Understanding the collection phase underscores the critical need for robust security measures to safeguard sensitive information. As cyber threats evolve, defenders must employ a combination of proactive security solutions, continuous monitoring, and rapid incident response to mitigate the risks associated with data collection by malicious actors.

CHAPTER 15

Code Pollution: Tainting the Digital Canvas

Code pollution represents a sophisticated and insidious form of cyber-attack where adversaries introduce malicious elements into source code repositories or manipulate scripts and binaries during the build process. This phase of an attack undermines the integrity of software development, posing severe threats to the security and reliability of applications.

1. Injecting Malicious Code into Source Code Repositories:

How It Works: Stealthy Contamination of Code Bases

Adversaries discreetly inject malicious code snippets or backdoors into source code repositories. This can be achieved through unauthorised access to version control systems or by exploiting vulnerabilities in the development environment.

Examples: EventStream NPM Package (2018)

In the EventStream incident of 2018, an attacker injected malicious code into a popular JavaScript library (NPM package) used by the event-stream module. This led to the compromise of downstream applications that incorporated the tainted package.

Discovery: Code Review and Dependency Scanning

Code pollution through injected malicious code can be discovered through thorough code reviews and automated dependency scanning tools. These mechanisms identify anomalies, suspicious functions, or unexpected changes in the codebase.

Impacts: Compromised Software Supply Chain and Backdoored Applications

The compromise of source code repositories can result in the distribution of tainted software components, creating a ripple effect across the software supply chain. Applications relying on these compromised components may unknowingly introduce security vulnerabilities or backdoors.

2. Manipulating Scripts or Binaries During the Build Process:

How It Works: Undermining Build Integrity

Adversaries manipulate build scripts or binaries during the build process, introducing malicious alterations before the final application is created. This can involve tampering with build configurations, introducing unauthorised dependencies, or injecting malicious code into compiled binaries.

Examples: Compromised SolarWinds Orion Build (2020)

In the SolarWinds supply chain attack of 2020, threat actors manipulated the build process of the SolarWinds Orion software. By introducing a malicious DLL (Dynamic Link Library) during the build, they orchestrated a widespread compromise of organisations using the compromised software.

Discovery: Build Integrity Checks and Continuous Monitoring

Detecting manipulations during the build process requires rigorous build integrity checks and continuous monitoring. Deviation from established build configurations, unexpected alterations to binaries, or

the presence of unauthorised components are indicators of potential manipulation.

Impacts: Trojanised Software Distribution and Backdoored Deployments

Manipulating scripts or binaries during the build process can result in the distribution of trojanised software or the deployment of applications with built-in backdoors. The impacts extend to compromised systems, unauthorised access, and potential data breaches.

3. Other Techniques:

 - Dependency Confusion Attacks: Uploading malicious packages to public or private repositories with names similar to legitimate dependencies.

 - Compiler-Based Attacks: Manipulating the compiler itself to introduce malicious code during the compilation process.

 - Backdooring Frameworks: Introducing vulnerabilities or malicious components into popular frameworks used by developers.

Detection and Mitigation:

 - Integrity Verification: Implementing cryptographic hashes and digital signatures to verify the integrity of source code and binaries.

 - Build Pipeline Security: Securing the build pipeline with access controls, monitoring, and validation mechanisms.

 - Static and Dynamic Analysis: Employing static analysis tools and dynamic analysis during runtime to identify and mitigate code pollution.

Takeaway for the Reader:

Code pollution attacks emphasise the critical importance of securing the software development lifecycle. Developers and organisations must implement robust security practices, including code reviews, dependency scanning, and build integrity checks, to safeguard against the introduction of malicious elements into the codebase. Awareness of these sophisticated attack techniques is essential for maintaining the trustworthiness of software supply chains and protecting end-users from potentially harmful applications.

CHAPTER 16

Command and Control: Orchestrating the Symphony of Intrusion

Command and Control (C2) represents a crucial phase in cyber-attacks where adversaries establish covert communication channels to maintain control over compromised systems. Techniques in this phase include the creation of stealthy communication pathways and the use of covert methods like DNS tunnelling for command and control.

1. Establishing Covert Communication Channels:

How It Works: Concealing Communication for Control

Adversaries create covert communication channels to discreetly exchange commands and exfiltrate data from compromised systems. This involves evading traditional network monitoring tools and disguising malicious traffic within seemingly legitimate communications.

Real-Life Example: Zeus Gameover Botnet

The Zeus Gameover botnet, a variant of the Zeus Trojan, utilised a peer-to-peer (P2P) communication

model for its C2 infrastructure. This decentralised approach made it more challenging for security analysts to identify and dismantle the botnet's command and control capabilities.

Detection: Anomaly Detection and Behavioural Analysis

Detecting covert communication channels involves anomaly detection and behavioural analysis. Deviations from normal network patterns, unexpected data flows, or communication with known malicious entities can indicate the presence of covert C2 channels.

Impacts: Persistent Control and Data Exfiltration

Successful establishment of covert communication channels allows adversaries to maintain persistent control over compromised systems. The impacts include the potential for ongoing malicious activities, data exfiltration, and the execution of additional commands without detection.

2. Using DNS Tunnelling for Command and Control:

How It Works: Riding the DNS Protocol for Stealth

DNS tunnelling involves embedding command and control messages within DNS queries and responses. Adversaries exploit the DNS protocol's ubiquity and the likelihood of organisations allowing DNS traffic to pass through firewalls without thorough inspection.

Real-Life Example: FIN7 Carbanak Campaign

The FIN7 cybercriminal group, known for the Carbanak malware campaign, utilised DNS tunnelling to communicate with their command and control servers. This technique allowed them to maintain a low profile by leveraging legitimate DNS traffic for malicious purposes.

Detection: DNS Traffic Analysis and Pattern Recognition

Detecting DNS tunnelling involves thorough analysis of DNS traffic, looking for patterns indicative of abnormal behaviour. Unusual query/response patterns, large amounts of data transferred through DNS, or repeated queries to uncommon domains are potential indicators.

Impacts: Covert Communication and Evasion of Detection Mechanisms

DNS tunnelling enables covert communication, allowing adversaries to bypass traditional security mechanisms that might inspect and block other types of traffic. This evasion capability increases the likelihood of maintaining persistence within a compromised network.

3. Other Techniques:

 - HTTP-based C2: Using HTTP protocols to communicate with command and control servers.

 - IP-based Communication: Direct communication between compromised systems and external servers via IP addresses.

 - Use of Legitimate Services: Leveraging well-known cloud services for command and control to blend in with legitimate traffic.

Mitigation and Detection:

 - DNS Traffic Monitoring: Implementing DNS traffic monitoring to identify unusual patterns and potential tunnelling.

- Behavioural Anomalies: Employing behavioural analysis to detect deviations from normal network behaviour.

- Threat Intelligence Integration: Utilising threat intelligence feeds to identify known malicious domains or IP addresses associated with C2 infrastructure.

Takeaway for the Reader:

Understanding the intricacies of command and control techniques highlights the critical role of robust network monitoring and anomaly detection in cybersecurity. Organisations must stay vigilant, employ advanced threat detection mechanisms, and integrate threat intelligence to thwart the covert orchestration of cyber intrusions. The ability to recognise and respond to C2 activities is paramount in minimising the potential impact of a cyber-attack.

CHAPTER 17

Exfiltration: Unveiling the Silent Escape

Exfiltration marks the stage where adversaries stealthily steal sensitive data from compromised systems, manoeuvring through encrypted channels and concealing their activities within common protocols. This phase poses a significant threat to the confidentiality and integrity of valuable information.

1. Stealing Sensitive Data Through Encrypted Channels:

How It Operates: Concealed Data Transfer for Secrecy

Adversaries leverage encrypted channels to steal sensitive data, ensuring that their exfiltration activities remain hidden from traditional network monitoring. Encryption adds an extra layer of obfuscation, making it challenging for defenders to detect the theft of confidential information.

What It Looks Like: Unusual Outbound Traffic and Encrypted Payloads

Detecting exfiltration through encrypted channels involves monitoring for unusual patterns of outbound traffic, particularly if it is encrypted. Encrypted payloads

within the network may be indicative of data exfiltration, especially if the encryption is not typical for the monitored network.

Defence Actions: Deep Packet Inspection and Anomaly Detection

Defending against exfiltration through encrypted channels requires deep packet inspection capable of analysing encrypted traffic. Anomaly detection mechanisms can identify deviations from baseline communication patterns, triggering alerts for further investigation.

Repercussions: Data Exposure and Privacy Violations

Successful exfiltration through encrypted channels can lead to the exposure of sensitive data. The repercussions extend to potential privacy violations, regulatory penalties, and reputational damage for organisations entrusted with safeguarding confidential information.

2. Covert Channels Within Common Protocols:

How It Works: Concealing Data in Plain Sight

Adversaries embed exfiltration activities within common and seemingly innocuous network protocols. By exploiting the inherent trust associated with widely used communication methods, they covertly transfer sensitive data without raising suspicion.

What It Looks Like: Anomalies in Protocol Usage and Unusual Data Patterns

Detecting covert channels within common protocols involves monitoring for anomalies in protocol usage. Unusual data patterns or unexpected variations in the volume and frequency of communication may indicate the presence of covert exfiltration activities.

Defence Actions: Protocol Analysis and Pattern Recognition

Defending against covert channels within common protocols requires protocol analysis tools capable of identifying deviations from normal communication behaviour. Pattern recognition algorithms can assist in pinpointing irregularities that may signal covert data exfiltration.

Repercussions: Undetected Data Theft and Extended Compromise

Covert channels within common protocols enable adversaries to exfiltrate data discreetly, potentially prolonging their compromise of the target environment. Extended compromise increases the likelihood of additional malicious activities and persistent access to sensitive information.

3. Other Techniques:

- DNS Exfiltration: Using DNS queries to transmit stolen data, often through subdomains or TXT records.

- Steganography: Concealing data within seemingly innocuous files, images, or other digital media.

- Data Fragmentation: Breaking down stolen data into smaller fragments to avoid detection.

Mitigation and Detection:

- Endpoint Monitoring: Implementing endpoint detection and response (EDR) solutions to identify anomalous data transfer patterns.

- Behavioural Analysis: Utilising behavioural analytics to detect deviations from normal user and system behaviour.

- Data Loss Prevention (DLP): Employing DLP solutions to monitor and control the movement of sensitive data.

Takeaway for the Reader:

Understanding the intricacies of exfiltration techniques underscores the importance of a multi-layered defence strategy. Organisations must implement robust endpoint monitoring, behavioural analysis, and DLP measures to detect and mitigate the theft of sensitive data. By staying informed about the methods employed by adversaries, defenders can enhance their ability to safeguard critical information and mitigate the potential impact of data exfiltration.

CHAPTER 18

Impact: Unravelling the Aftermath of Cyber Attacks

The impact phase of a cyber-attack reveals the tangible consequences, ranging from the well-known, such as ransomware encrypting data and DDoS attacks disrupting services, to lesser-known but equally destructive tactics. This stage lays bare the financial, operational, and reputational fallout that organisations face in the wake of a successful breach.

1. Ransomware Attacks Causing Data Encryption:

Well-Known Example: WannaCry (2017)

WannaCry, a notorious ransomware variant, encrypted data on infected systems and demanded payment in cryptocurrency for decryption keys. The attack affected organisations globally, including healthcare facilities and government institutions, showcasing the widespread impact of ransomware.

Lesser-Known Example: Ryuk (2019)

Ryuk, a sophisticated ransomware strain, gained notoriety for targeting high-profile organisations and demanding hefty ransoms. Its advanced capabilities included the ability to identify and encrypt critical files, causing significant disruption and financial losses for the victims.

Costs and Losses: Ransom Payments, Remediation, and Downtime

The costs of ransomware attacks extend beyond the ransom payments. Organisations incur expenses for incident response, system remediation, and downtime during the recovery process. Additionally, the reputational damage from such incidents can have long-term financial repercussions.

2. DDoS Attacks Disrupting Services:

Well-Known Example: Mirai Botnet (2016)

The Mirai botnet orchestrated massive DDoS attacks by compromising Internet of Things (IoT) devices. The attacks targeted critical internet infrastructure, leading to widespread service disruptions. Mirai demonstrated the vulnerability of IoT devices and their potential use as weapons in large-scale DDoS attacks.

Lesser-Known Example: GitHub (2018)

In 2018, GitHub experienced one of the largest DDoS attacks in history, surpassing 1.35 terabits per second. The attack utilised a technique called amplification, leveraging misconfigured Memcached servers to magnify the volume of traffic directed at GitHub's infrastructure, causing temporary service unavailability.

Costs and Losses: Downtime, Bandwidth Costs, and Reputation Damage

DDoS attacks result in direct financial losses due to increased bandwidth costs and potential service downtime. The impact on an organisation's reputation can be substantial, especially if customers or users experience disruptions or outages.

3. Other Techniques and Lesser-Known Facts:

- Fileless Malware Attacks: Malicious code that operates in memory, leaving fewer traces and evading traditional antivirus solutions.

- Watering Hole Attacks: Compromising websites frequented by a target audience to distribute malware.

- Business Email Compromise (BEC): Manipulating employees into transferring funds or sensitive information through fraudulent email communication.

Additional Facts and Considerations:

 - Third-Party Risks: Cybersecurity risks extend beyond an organisation's immediate control, emphasising the importance of assessing and mitigating risks associated with third-party vendors and partners.

 - Regulatory Consequences: Non-compliance with data protection regulations can result in significant fines and legal consequences, compounding the impact of a cyber-attack.

 - Proactive Defence Strategies: Organisations should adopt proactive defence strategies, including threat intelligence sharing, employee training, and regular security assessments, to reduce the likelihood and impact of cyber-attacks.

Takeaway for the Reader:

Understanding the varied impacts of cyber-attacks reinforces the necessity of a holistic cybersecurity approach. Organisations must not only defend against immediate threats but also anticipate and mitigate the potential fallout. By staying informed about both well-known and lesser-known tactics, defenders can fortify their cybersecurity posture and minimise the financial, operational, and reputational impact of cyber incidents.

CHAPTER 19

Cyber Futures: Navigating the Quantum Era and Evolving Security Landscape

As we peer into the next decade and beyond, the realm of cybersecurity stands at a crossroads, shaped by emerging technologies, evolving threats, and the transformative power of quantum computing. The future promises both challenges and opportunities, prompting a re-evaluation of security paradigms and the adoption of innovative defences.

1. Quantum Computers: Revolutionising Cryptography and Threat Landscape

Quantum Computing Breakthroughs:

The advent of quantum computers poses a fundamental shift in the cryptographic landscape. These powerful machines, leveraging the principles of quantum mechanics, have the potential to break widely-used encryption algorithms, rendering current security protocols obsolete.

Post-Quantum Cryptography:

The cybersecurity community is actively engaged in developing post-quantum cryptographic algorithms resilient to quantum attacks. Transitioning to these new encryption standards will be imperative to secure sensitive data in the quantum era.

Quantum Key Distribution (QKD):

Quantum key distribution offers a quantum-safe method for secure communication. By leveraging the principles of quantum entanglement, QKD allows parties to exchange cryptographic keys with a level of security that quantum computers cannot compromise.

2. Ciphering in the Evolving World of Cybersecurity

Zero-Trust Architectures:

Zero-trust architectures, emphasising the principle of "trust no one, verify everything," are gaining prominence. In this model, security is not solely reliant on perimeter defences; instead, every user and device is treated as potentially untrusted, necessitating continuous verification.

AI and Machine Learning Integration:

The integration of artificial intelligence (AI) and machine learning (ML) into cybersecurity operations is becoming more sophisticated. These technologies enhance threat detection, automate response mechanisms, and provide insights into evolving attack patterns.

Immutable Security:

The concept of immutable security revolves around creating systems that, once configured securely, remain unchanged and resistant to unauthorised modifications. This approach aims to minimise vulnerabilities and reduce the attack surface available to malicious actors.

3. What to Consider in the Next Decade and Beyond

Interconnected Ecosystems:

With the rise of the Internet of Things (IoT) and the increasing connectivity of devices, securing interconnected ecosystems becomes paramount. Protecting not only traditional endpoints but also a multitude of IoT devices will be a critical focus.

Regulatory Landscape:

Anticipating and adapting to evolving cybersecurity regulations will be essential. Governments worldwide are placing a greater emphasis on data protection, and organisations must stay compliant with an evolving regulatory landscape.

Human Element:

Recognising the human element as a significant factor in cybersecurity is crucial. As technology advances, social engineering and human-centric attacks persist. Cybersecurity awareness, training, and the development of a cyber-resilient culture within organisations are vital.

Global Collaboration:

Cyber threats are borderless, and global collaboration is essential. Information sharing between organisations, industries, and nations is crucial for early threat detection and effective response.

Continual Innovation:

The pace of technological innovation demands continual adaptation. Cybersecurity professionals must

stay ahead of emerging threats, continuously innovate their defence strategies, and be prepared to embrace new technologies and methodologies.

The Future is Dynamic: A Call to Proactive Cyber Resilience

As we venture into the next ten years and beyond, the future of cybersecurity is dynamic and shaped by the interplay of technological advancements, threat evolution, and the resilience of defenders. Embracing a proactive approach, organisations and cybersecurity professionals can fortify their defences, navigate the quantum era, and secure the digital landscapes of tomorrow. The journey ahead demands continual vigilance, collaboration, and a commitment to cyber resilience in the face of an ever-evolving cyber landscape.

CHAPTER 20

Securing the Digital Frontier: A Comprehensive Summary

In the ever-evolving landscape of cybersecurity, the past, present, and future converge to paint a complex tapestry of challenges and innovations. From risk scoring in contemporary threat landscapes to the intricacies of cyber warfare and the looming quantum era, the journey through the digital frontier demands resilience, adaptability, and a keen understanding of emerging paradigms.

1. Contemporary Cybersecurity Risk Scoring:

 - Anonymisation and Threat Vectors: Striking a balance between privacy and security is crucial. Anonymisation practices must align with the evolving threat landscape.

 - Medium to High Risk Areas: Cyberfraud, data leakage, service disruption, and vendor risks present considerable challenges. Vigilance in these areas is paramount.

2. Cybersecurity Risk Scenarios and Ratings:

- Comprehensive Scenarios: From open-source intelligence gathering to phishing attacks, the scenarios span the cyber threat spectrum.

- Varied Risk Ratings: The risks vary from low to very high, emphasising the dynamic nature of cyber threats and the need for nuanced defence strategies.

3. Crafting "Cyber wise" – A Comprehensive Cybersecurity Guide:

- Structured Approach: "Cyber wise" delves into the intricacies of the cyber kill chain, guiding readers through reconnaissance to impact with real-world examples.

- Empowering Defenders: By unravelling the tactics, techniques, and procedures (TTPs) of adversaries, "Cyber wise" empowers defenders with knowledge to thwart cyber threats.

4. Historical Perspective on Cybersecurity:

- Genesis of Cybersecurity: From the ARPANET era to the Stuxnet worm, the historical narrative underscores the transformative journey of cybersecurity.

- Stepping Stones: Key milestones, such as the development of encryption algorithms and the rise of ethical hacking, paved the way for modern cybersecurity practices.

5. Reconnaissance in the Digital Battlefield:

- OSINT and Beyond: Open-source intelligence (OSINT) through social media, DNS enumeration, and network scanning are critical reconnaissance techniques.

- Real-Time Examples: The inclusion of up-to-date examples highlights the relevance of these techniques in contemporary cyber threats.

6. Resource Development and its Impacts:

- Domain Squatting: Techniques like domain squatting and typosquatting have tangible impacts on phishing campaigns.

- Employee Information Exposure: Scraping websites for employee information poses risks and necessitates robust defences.

7. Initial Access and the Seeds of Intrusion:

 - Phishing Attacks: Spear-phishing emails remain a potent initial access vector, emphasising the importance of user awareness.

 - Software Vulnerabilities: Exploiting unpatched systems demonstrates the need for proactive patch management.

8. Execution and the Unleashing of Malicious Payloads:

 - Malware Execution: Through malicious attachments, adversaries compromise systems and elevate the threat landscape.

 - Web Application Attacks: Code injection targeting web applications underscores the diversity of execution techniques.

9. Persistence in the Shadows:

 - Backdoors and Registry Persistence: Adversaries leverage backdoors and registry persistence, necessitating continuous monitoring.

 - Indicators of Compromise: Identifying these indicators is crucial for early detection and response.

10. Privilege Escalation: Scaling the Heights of Access:

 - Misconfigurations and Weak Permissions: Exploiting misconfigurations and weak permissions highlights the necessity of robust access controls.

 - Detection and Prevention: Recognising common techniques and implementing detection mechanisms are pivotal.

11. Defence Evasion Tactics: Navigating Stealthily:

 - Signature Evasion: Polymorphic malware exemplifies the cat-and-mouse game of signature evasion.

 - Disabling Security Software: The disabling of security software underscores the need for resilient defence measures.

12. Credential Access and the Hunt for Digital Keys:

 - Password Spraying and Keylogging: Password spraying attacks and keylogging showcase the diverse methods employed for credential access.

 - Defensive Measures: Multi-factor authentication (MFA) and vigilant monitoring are crucial defences against credential-based threats.

13. Discovery: Unveiling the Digital Landscape:

 - Active Directory Reconnaissance: Understanding the importance of Active Directory reconnaissance is foundational to defence.

 - Network Mapping: Techniques like network mapping necessitate continual monitoring for early threat detection.

14. Lateral Movement: Manoeuvring Within Networks:

 - Exploiting Trust Relationships: Exploiting trust relationships underscores the necessity of zero-trust architectures.

 - Compromised Credentials: The use of compromised credentials emphasises the need for robust identity and access management.

15. Collection: Harvesting the Digital Bounty:

 - Covert Data Exfiltration: Covert channels for data exfiltration, as seen in Stuxnet and SolarWinds, require vigilant monitoring.

 - Harvesting Sensitive Information: Direct harvesting from compromised systems exemplifies the broad impact of collection techniques.

16. Impact: The Tangible Fallout of Cyber Attacks (Continued):

 - Ransomware and DDoS (Continued): ...of cyber-attacks. Beyond WannaCry and the Mirai botnet, ransomware and DDoS attacks cause financial losses, service disruptions, and reputational damage.

 - Costs and Losses: The financial toll of ransom payments, incident response, and downtime amplifies the overall costs. DDoS-induced downtime and bandwidth costs compound the impact, underscoring the multifaceted consequences.

17. Cyber Futures: Navigating Uncharted Territory:

 - Quantum Computers: The advent of quantum computing introduces a paradigm shift, challenging traditional cryptographic methods. The pursuit of post-quantum cryptography and quantum key distribution emerges as a crucial defence.

 - Evolving Ciphering Strategies: Zero-trust architectures, AI and ML integration, and the concept of immutable security redefine the approach to cyber defences. The dynamic interplay of these strategies strengthens resilience against evolving threats.

18. What to Consider in the Next Decade and Beyond:

- Interconnected Ecosystems: The proliferation of IoT devices demands a holistic approach to security. Protecting interconnected ecosystems involves securing traditional endpoints and diverse IoT devices.

- Regulatory Landscape: Adapting to evolving cybersecurity regulations is paramount. Organisations must stay compliant to avoid legal consequences and reputational damage.

- Human Element: Recognising the human factor as a significant vulnerability is crucial. Cybersecurity awareness, training, and a culture of cyber resilience are essential defences against social engineering attacks.

- Global Collaboration: The borderless nature of cyber threats necessitates global collaboration. Information sharing between organisations and nations enhances threat detection and response capabilities.

- Continual Innovation: The rapid pace of technological innovation requires continuous adaptation. Staying ahead of emerging threats demands proactive defence strategies, threat intelligence integration, and embracing new technologies.

Conclusion: Navigating the Cyber Landscape with Wisdom and Vigilance

As we summarise the multifaceted journey through the cyber landscape, it becomes evident that the future of cybersecurity is a dynamic tapestry woven with innovation, challenges, and resilience. From historical milestones to contemporary risk scenarios and future considerations, the narrative underscores the need for a holistic approach to defence.

The main considerations for the next decade and beyond involve embracing new cryptographic paradigms, fortifying defences against quantum threats, and adopting evolving strategies like zero-trust architectures and AI-driven security. Interconnected ecosystems, regulatory compliance, human-centric defences, global collaboration, and a commitment to continual innovation are pivotal for navigating the uncharted territories of cyber futures.

In the face of evolving threats, the wisdom lies in proactive cyber resilience — a continual commitment to learning, adapting, and collaborating. With knowledge as the guiding compass, organisations and cybersecurity professionals can navigate the ever-changing cyber landscape with wisdom and vigilance, ensuring a secure digital future for all.

A note from the author.

Thank you for reading. Please share with any and all of your friends.

Also if you are feeling the urge – then please write a review, that way I can figure out what we need to provide in any future writings.

Kind regards R. Allure